Muhammad Ajmal
Akhter Habib Shah

A Resource Book for School Children

Muhammad Ajmal
Akhter Habib Shah

A Resource Book for School Children

Make Students Learn from Stories in Classroom

JustFiction Edition

Imprint

Any brand names and product names mentioned in this book are subject to trademark, brand or patent protection and are trademarks or registered trademarks of their respective holders. The use of brand names, product names, common names, trade names, product descriptions etc. even without a particular marking in this work is in no way to be construed to mean that such names may be regarded as unrestricted in respect of trademark and brand protection legislation and could thus be used by anyone.

Cover image: www.ingimage.com

Publisher:
JustFiction! Edition
is a trademark of
Dodo Books Indian Ocean Ltd. and OmniScriptum S.R.L publishing group

120 High Road, East Finchley, London, N2 9ED, United Kingdom
Str. Armeneasca 28/1, office 1, Chisinau MD-2012, Republic of Moldova, Europe
Printed at: see last page
ISBN: 978-620-0-10640-7

A Resource Book for School Children

(Make Students Learn from Stories in Classroom)

By

Muhammad Ajmal

Akhter Habib Shah

Preface

Dear Reader,

It is our pleasure to introduce this book of stories for young learners of Grade-5-8. As teachers and writers, we understand the importance of engaging young minds with stories that relate to their lives. They can inspire us, teach us, and help us understand the world around us. That's why we've written this collection of stories that focus on topics that young learners can relate to, such as friendship, family, school, and everyday experiences. That's why we're thrilled to introduce this anthology of short stories for children with more purpose.

The stories in this collection are more than just entertainment. Each one has been carefully crafted to help children learn important lessons, build their empathy, and develop their emotional intelligence. They cover a wide range of topics, from forgiveness and friendship to diversity and inclusion, and are suitable for children of all ages.

As a teacher or parent, you can use these stories to start conversations with young learners about important topics that affect their lives. They can help children develop their social skills, emotional intelligence, and empathy towards others. Exercise at the end of each story will make the student(s) more cautious and attentive while reading the text.

We hope that this book of stories will bring joy and inspiration to young readers, and serve as a valuable resource for parents, caregivers, and educators. Thank you for choosing this book, and we hope you enjoy reading these stories as much as we enjoyed writing them.

Sincerely,

Muhammad Ajmal

Akhter Habib Shah

Table of Content

The Bird

Once upon a time, there was a small bird named Pip. Pip lived in a cozy nest high up in a tree in the middle of a beautiful forest. Every day, Pip would wake up at dawn and fly around the forest, singing beautiful songs to all the animals that lived there. Everyone loved Pip, and they would always stop and listen to the beautiful melodies.

One day, while Pip was flying around, admiring the beautiful scenery, he noticed something strange. In the distance, he saw a group of birds flying towards him. At first, Pip thought they were just passing by, but as they got closer, he realized they were coming straight towards him. Before he could react, they swooped down and attacked him, pecking and clawing at him until he fell to the ground.

Pip was badly hurt, and he lay there, helpless, for what felt like an eternity. Finally, a kind-hearted squirrel came to his rescue and took him to her cozy burrow. She tended to Pip's wounds and nursed him back to health, but he was never the same. He had lost his confidence and his beautiful singing voice.

As time went by, Pip watched from a distance as the other birds continued to sing and fly freely in the forest. He longed to join them, but he was too afraid. One day, he decided he couldn't let fear control his life anymore, and he slowly started to build up his confidence again. He practiced singing in his burrow until he was ready to show the other animals his beautiful voice.

One sunny day, Pip flew out of his burrow and soared high into the sky. He sang the most beautiful song he had ever sung, and all the animals in the forest stopped to listen. They were amazed by the beautiful melody, and they cheered and clapped when Pip finished.

From that day on, Pip became known as the bravest and most talented bird in the forest. He had conquered his fears and had become an inspiration to all the animals in the forest. And every day, he would fly around, singing his beautiful songs, spreading joy and happiness wherever he went.

Exercise

Select 3 words which are new for you in the story and make sentences in your own words.

    1) ____

    2) ____

    3) ____

Identify 2 adjectives and 2 adverbs used in the story.

Adjectives: ________________ ________________ ________________

Adverbs: ________________ ________________ ________________

Write 3 sentences about the main character in your own words.

    1) ____

    2) ____

    3) ____

What was the main idea of the story?

Reply:____
____

What was the problem faced by the main character in the story? How was it resolved?

Reply:____
____

Find two examples of similes or metaphors used in the story. Explain what they mean.

Reply:____
____

If you were the author, how would you change the ending of the story? Why?

Reply:____
____
____
____

The Donkey

In a small village nestled in the hills, there lived a hardworking donkey named Jack. Jack belonged to a poor farmer who depended on him to carry heavy loads of crops to the market every week. Despite his tired and overworked state, Jack never complained, as he knew his work was essential for his owner's livelihood.

One day, while on his way to the market, Jack met a group of young donkeys who were frolicking in a nearby field. They laughed and played, completely carefree. Jack felt a pang of envy as he watched them, wishing he too could enjoy such a life of leisure.

The young donkeys noticed Jack's sad expression and asked him what was wrong. Jack replied, "I am envious of your carefree life. I have to work hard every day, carrying heavy loads to the market, while you get to play and enjoy yourselves."

The young donkeys were surprised by Jack's response and asked him why he didn't just run away and live a carefree life like them. Jack replied, "I cannot leave my owner in need. He depends on me, and I must do my part to ensure his family's livelihood. My work may be hard, but it is honorable and necessary."

The young donkeys were inspired by Jack's dedication and sense of responsibility. They realized that there was more to life than just having fun and being carefree. They too wanted to make a difference in the world.

From that day on, the young donkeys started helping Jack with his work. They carried smaller loads and assisted him with the heavy lifting, making his work easier and more manageable. In return, Jack taught them the importance of responsibility and hard work.

Together, they became a team, and their combined efforts helped the farmer's family prosper. And although Jack still had to work hard every day, he no longer felt envious of the young donkeys. He had found a sense of fulfillment and purpose in his work and had inspired a group of young animals to make a difference in the world.

Exercise

Select 3 words which are new for you in the story and make sentences in your own words.

    1) ____

    2) ____

    3) ____

Identify 2 adjectives and 2 adverbs used in the story.

Adjectives: ______________ ______________ ______________

Adverbs: ______________ ______________ ______________

Write 3 sentences about the main character in your own words.

    1) ____

    2) ____

    3) ____

What was the main idea of the story?

Reply:____

____

What was the problem faced by the main character in the story? How was it resolved?

Reply:____

____

Find two examples of similes or metaphors used in the story. Explain what they mean.

Reply:____

____

If you were the author, how would you change the ending of the story? Why?

Reply:____

____

____

____

The Doctor

Dr. Sarah was a dedicated and compassionate doctor who had been practicing medicine for over twenty years. She had a small clinic in a remote village, where she treated patients from all walks of life, regardless of their ability to pay.

One day, a young girl named Maya was brought to Dr. Sarah's clinic. Maya was gravely ill and needed immediate medical attention. Dr. Sarah worked tirelessly to save her, but despite her best efforts, Maya's condition continued to deteriorate. Dr. Sarah knew that she needed specialized care and referred her to a hospital in the city.

However, the hospital was miles away, and Maya's family could not afford the transportation costs. Dr. Sarah could not bear to see Maya suffer any longer and decided to take matters into her own hands. She packed her medical bag, arranged for a ride, and accompanied Maya and her family to the hospital.

Dr. Sarah stayed with Maya and her family at the hospital, ensuring that she received the best possible care. She spent hours talking to the doctors and nurses, making sure they were doing everything they could to save Maya's life. She comforted Maya's family, assuring them that they were not alone in this fight.

After several weeks, Maya's condition stabilized, and she began to recover. Dr. Sarah stayed by her side until she was well enough to go home. She then returned to her clinic in the village, where she continued to care for her patients with the same level of dedication and compassion as before.

Months later, Dr. Sarah received a letter from Maya's family, thanking her for her selfless act of kindness. They wrote that Maya had made a full recovery and was now living a healthy and happy life. The letter was a reminder to Dr. Sarah of why she became a doctor in the first place: to make a positive impact on people's lives and to provide hope in times of despair.

Dr. Sarah continued to practice medicine for many years, always going above and beyond to help those in need. She never forgot the lessons she learned from Maya and her family, and their gratitude served as a constant reminder that even the smallest act of kindness can make a world of difference.

Exercise

Select 3 words which are new for you in the story and make sentences in your own words.

    1) ____

    2) ____

    3) ____

Identify 2 adjectives and 2 adverbs used in the story.

Adjectives: ________________ ________________ ________________

Adverbs: ________________ ________________ ________________

Write 3 sentences about the main character in your own words.

    1) ____

    2) ____

    3) ____

What was the main idea of the story?

Reply:____

____

What was the problem faced by the main character in the story? How was it resolved?

Reply:____

____

Find two examples of similes or metaphors used in the story. Explain what they mean.

Reply:____

____

If you were the author, how would you change the ending of the story? Why?

Reply:____

____

____

____

The Eldest Sister

Lila was the eldest of three sisters. She had always been responsible and mature beyond her years, taking care of her younger siblings while their parents worked long hours to provide for their family.

Growing up, Lila never complained about her responsibilities. She understood that her parents needed to work to put food on the table, and she was happy to help out. However, as she got older, she began to feel the weight of her responsibilities more heavily.

While her sisters were out playing with their friends, Lila would be at home, cleaning the house, doing laundry, and cooking dinner. She felt like she was missing out on her childhood, but she never let her feelings show. She continued to take care of her sisters, always putting their needs before her own.

One day, Lila's parents sat her down and told her that they were moving to another city for work. They explained that they would need to leave Lila in charge of her sisters, as they would not be able to take them with them. Lila was terrified. She had never been alone with her sisters for more than a few hours, let alone for an extended period.

The first few days were tough. Lila struggled to keep up with all of the household chores while also taking care of her sisters' emotional needs. But slowly, she began to find her groove. She set up a schedule for herself and her sisters, making sure that they had time for homework, play, and relaxation.

As the weeks turned into months, Lila realized that she was more than capable of taking care of her sisters. She had become a second mother to them, providing love, support, and guidance when they needed it most. Her sisters looked up to her and respected her, and Lila felt a sense of pride knowing that she had been able to step up and take care of them when they needed her most.

When her parents returned, they were amazed at how well Lila had done. They praised her for her maturity and responsibility, telling her how proud they were of her. Lila smiled, knowing that she had proven to herself and her family that she was more than just the eldest sister. She was a caretaker, a leader, and a role model. And she was proud of who she had become.

Exercise

Select 3 words which are new for you in the story and make sentences in your own words.

    1) ____

    2) ____

    3) ____

Identify 2 adjectives and 2 adverbs used in the story.

Adjectives: ______________ ________________ ____________________

Adverbs: ______________ ________________ ____________________

Write 3 sentences about the main character in your own words.

    1) ____

    2) ____

    3) ____

What was the main idea of the story?

Reply:____

____

What was the problem faced by the main character in the story? How was it resolved?

Reply:____

____

Find two examples of similes or metaphors used in the story. Explain what they mean.

Reply:____

____

If you were the author, how would you change the ending of the story? Why?

Reply:____

____

____

____

The Gardener

Sam had always loved gardening. He loved the smell of fresh earth, the sound of birds singing, and the feeling of the sun on his skin. When he retired from his job as a bank manager, he decided to pursue his passion for gardening full-time.

Sam's garden was the envy of the neighborhood. He had rows upon rows of vegetables, fruits, and flowers, all meticulously tended to with care and attention. He spent hours in his garden every day, watering, pruning, and weeding, and he loved every minute of it.

One day, a young boy named Timmy came to Sam's door, asking if he could help him with his garden. Timmy explained that he had always been interested in gardening but didn't know where to start. Sam saw a spark in Timmy's eyes and knew that he could help him.

Sam took Timmy under his wing, showing him the basics of gardening and helping him plant his first garden. Timmy was a quick learner, and soon he was spending as much time in his garden as Sam did in his. Sam was proud of Timmy's progress, and he continued to mentor him, sharing tips and advice as they worked side by side in their gardens.

As the years passed, Sam's health began to decline, and he was no longer able to tend to his garden as he once had. But he knew that Timmy was more than capable of taking over. He handed over the reins to Timmy, trusting him to continue the work he had started.

Timmy took on the responsibility with pride, knowing that he had big shoes to fill. He tended to Sam's garden with the same care and attention that Sam had shown to him, and he continued to learn and grow as a gardener.

When Sam passed away, the entire neighborhood came to pay their respects. They talked about how Sam had been more than just a gardener, he had been a mentor, a friend, and a role model. They talked about the impact he had made on their lives and how grateful they were to have known him.

As Timmy tended to Sam's garden, he felt a sense of pride and gratitude. He knew that Sam's legacy would live on through the garden, and that he had a responsibility to carry on the work that Sam had started. And he was honored to do so, knowing that he had big shoes to fill, but also knowing that he had a mentor who had taught him everything he needed to know.

Exercise

Select 3 words which are new for you in the story and make sentences in your own words.

1) ____

2) ____

3) ____

Identify 2 adjectives and 2 adverbs used in the story.

Adjectives: ________________ ________________ ________________

Adverbs: ________________ ________________ ________________

Write 3 sentences about the main character in your own words.

1) ____

2) ____

3) ____

What was the main idea of the story?

Reply:____

____

What was the problem faced by the main character in the story? How was it resolved?

Reply:____

____

Find two examples of similes or metaphors used in the story. Explain what they mean.

Reply:____

____

If you were the author, how would you change the ending of the story? Why?

Reply:____

____

____

____

The Cat

Mittens was a small, fluffy cat with bright green eyes and a playful spirit. She lived in a cozy little house with her owner, Mary. Mittens loved Mary and would follow her around the house, meowing for attention whenever she could.

One day, Mary decided to adopt another cat named Tiger. Tiger was big and strong, with thick orange fur and a loud, booming meow. Mittens was unsure about the new addition to the household, and she kept her distance from Tiger at first.

But as the days went on, Mittens and Tiger began to get to know each other. They would play together, chasing each other around the house and wrestling on the living room rug. Mittens was surprised to find that she actually enjoyed Tiger's company, and she began to see him as a friend rather than an intruder.

One day, Mary noticed that Mittens had stopped eating and seemed to be lethargic. She took her to the vet, who diagnosed her with an infection. Mittens had to stay at the vet's office for a few days to receive treatment, and Mary was worried about her.

When Mittens came back home, she was weak and tired. But Tiger was right there by her side, purring softly and licking her fur. Mittens felt comforted by Tiger's presence, and she snuggled up next to him, feeling safe and warm.

Over the next few days, Tiger continued to look after Mittens, bringing her toys to play with and keeping her company as she rested. Mittens began to recover, and soon she was back to her old self, chasing after Tiger and meowing for attention.

Mary was amazed at how much Tiger had helped Mittens recover. She knew that Mittens would have a lifelong friend in Tiger, and she was grateful for his presence in their lives.

From that day on, Mittens and Tiger were inseparable. They would curl up together on the couch, play together in the backyard, and look after each other when one of them wasn't feeling well. Mittens had learned that sometimes, the best friends come in unexpected packages, and she was grateful for the bond she had formed with Tiger.

Exercise

Select 3 words which are new for you in the story and make sentences in your own words.

    1) ____

    2) ____

    3) ____

Identify 2 adjectives and 2 adverbs used in the story.

Adjectives: ______________ ______________ ______________

Adverbs: ______________ ______________ ______________

Write 3 sentences about the main character in your own words.

    1) ____

    2) ____

    3) ____

What was the main idea of the story?

Reply:____

____

What was the problem faced by the main character in the story? How was it resolved?

Reply:____

____

Find two examples of similes or metaphors used in the story. Explain what they mean.

Reply:____

____

If you were the author, how would you change the ending of the story? Why?

Reply:____

____

____

____

The Teacher

Mrs. Taylor had been a teacher for over 30 years. She had taught generations of students and was known throughout the school district as one of the best teachers around. Her classroom was always full of energy and excitement, and her students looked forward to coming to school every day.

One day, a new student named John joined Mrs. Taylor's class. John was a shy and introverted child, and he had a difficult time making friends. He was nervous about starting at a new school, but Mrs. Taylor made him feel welcome from the very first day.

Mrs. Taylor noticed that John was struggling academically, and she made it her mission to help him catch up. She spent extra time with him after class, going over his homework and giving him extra assignments to practice his skills. John was amazed by how much Mrs. Taylor cared about his success, and he began to work harder than he ever had before.

As the school year went on, John began to thrive. He made friends with some of his classmates, and he started to excel academically. He even won a prize for a science project he had worked on with Mrs. Taylor.

At the end of the school year, Mrs. Taylor was recognized as the Teacher of the Year. Her students cheered and applauded as she received her award, but Mrs. Taylor knew that she couldn't have done it without them. She thanked each and every one of her students, including John, for their hard work and dedication throughout the year.

Years later, when John was all grown up, he returned to the school to visit Mrs. Taylor. He told her that she had been the inspiration for his success, and that he had become a teacher himself because of her. Mrs. Taylor was overjoyed to hear this, knowing that she had made a difference in John's life.

Mrs. Taylor retired shortly after John's visit, but her legacy lived on. She had taught hundreds of students over the years, and many of them had gone on to do great things. But for John, and for many others, Mrs. Taylor would always be remembered as the teacher who had changed their lives.

Exercise

Select 3 words which are new for you in the story and make sentences in your own words.

1) ____

2) ____

3) ____

Identify 2 adjectives and 2 adverbs used in the story.

Adjectives: ________________ ________________ ________________

Adverbs: ________________ ________________ ________________

Write 3 sentences about the main character in your own words.

1) ____

2) ____

3) ____

What was the main idea of the story?

Reply:____

____

What was the problem faced by the main character in the story? How was it resolved?

Reply:____

____

Find two examples of similes or metaphors used in the story. Explain what they mean.

Reply:____

____

If you were the author, how would you change the ending of the story? Why?

Reply:____

____

____

The Zoo

The zoo was a magical place filled with all sorts of exotic creatures. It was a popular attraction, and people came from all over the world to see the animals and learn about their habitats. The zookeepers took great pride in their work, caring for the animals and making sure they were healthy and happy.

One day, a group of school children visited the zoo on a field trip. They were excited to see the animals up close and learn about their behaviors. As they walked through the zoo, they saw everything from majestic lions to playful monkeys to slithering snakes.

But as they approached the reptile house, they noticed that something was wrong. One of the snakes had escaped from its enclosure and was slithering freely around the exhibit. The children were frightened, and the zookeepers sprang into action, trying to catch the snake before it could harm anyone.

The snake was fast and slippery, and it evaded capture for hours. But the zookeepers were determined, and they worked tirelessly to catch the snake and return it to its enclosure.

Finally, after a long day of searching, the snake was found hiding under a rock in the exhibit. The zookeepers carefully caught it and put it back in its enclosure, making sure that it was secure this time.

The school children watched in amazement as the zookeepers worked together to catch the snake. They realized that the zookeepers were true heroes, dedicating their lives to the care and protection of the animals in their care.

As the children left the zoo that day, they felt grateful for the experience and the lessons they had learned. They knew that the zoo was a special place, where animals were respected and cared for, and they vowed to do their part to protect the creatures of the world.

Exercise

Select 3 words which are new for you in the story and make sentences in your own words.

1) ____

2) ____

3) ____

Identify 2 adjectives and 2 adverbs used in the story.

Adjectives: ________________ ________________ ________________

Adverbs: ________________ ________________ ________________

Write 3 sentences about the main character in your own words.

1) ____

2) ____

3) ____

What was the main idea of the story?

Reply:____

____

What was the problem faced by the main character in the story? How was it resolved?

Reply:____

____

Find two examples of similes or metaphors used in the story. Explain what they mean.

Reply:____

____

If you were the author, how would you change the ending of the story? Why?

Reply:____

____

____

____

The Thief

Lena had always been a thief. Ever since she was a young girl, she had been stealing from shops and markets, trying to provide for her family. Her mother was sick, and her father had left them years ago, leaving Lena to take care of her younger siblings.

Lena's thievery had become more and more frequent over the years, as her family's needs grew and her desperation deepened. She knew it was wrong, but she felt like she had no other choice.

One day, Lena was caught stealing from a local market. The shopkeeper called the police, and Lena was taken away in handcuffs. She was terrified, knowing that she might be facing jail time.

But something unexpected happened during her trial. The judge, a kind-hearted woman named Maria, saw something in Lena that others had missed. She saw the pain in her eyes, the desperation in her actions. She knew that Lena needed help, not punishment.

So instead of sentencing Lena to jail, Judge Maria ordered her to perform community service. Lena was assigned to work at a local homeless shelter, where she spent her days helping those in need. She cooked meals, cleaned up, and listened to the stories of the people she met.

As she worked at the shelter, Lena began to feel a sense of purpose that she had never experienced before. She realized that she had been so focused on herself and her family's needs that she had forgotten about the needs of others. She saw that there were people out there who were much worse off than she was, and she wanted to do something to help them.

Over time, Lena's life began to change. She stopped stealing and started working hard to make an honest living. She volunteered at the shelter on weekends, and she even started taking classes to earn her high school diploma.

Years later, Lena looked back on her life and realized that her arrest had been a turning point. It had forced her to confront her actions and make a change for the better. She knew that she would always be grateful to Judge Maria for giving her a second chance, and she promised herself that she would never forget the lessons she had learned.

Exercise

Select 3 words which are new for you in the story and make sentences in your own words.

    1) ____

    2) ____

    3) ____

Identify 2 adjectives and 2 adverbs used in the story.

Adjectives: ______________   ______________   ______________

Adverbs: ______________   ______________   ______________

Write 3 sentences about the main character in your own words.

    1) ____

    2) ____

    3) ____

What was the main idea of the story?

Reply:____

____

What was the problem faced by the main character in the story? How was it resolved?

Reply:____

____

Find two examples of similes or metaphors used in the story. Explain what they mean.

Reply:____

____

If you were the author, how would you change the ending of the story? Why?

Reply:____

____

____

____

The School Bus Driver

Mrs. Wilson had been a school bus driver for over 20 years. She loved her job, and she loved the children she transported every day. To her, being a school bus driver wasn't just a job, it was a calling.

Mrs. Wilson was known for her kindness and her patience. She always greeted each child with a smile, and she made sure that everyone was safely buckled in before she started the bus. She drove carefully, always mindful of the precious cargo she carried.

One winter day, a blizzard hit the town, and school was canceled. But Mrs. Wilson knew that some children might still need to get to school, especially those whose parents had to work. So she decided to take matters into her own hands.

She got up early and shoveled the snow off her driveway, then bundled up in her warmest coat and hat. She drove to each stop on her route, even though no children were waiting, just to make sure that everyone knew that school was canceled. She left notes on each door, reminding parents to keep their children warm and safe.

As she drove, Mrs. Wilson noticed that some of the roads were treacherous, covered in snow and ice. She saw several cars slide off the road, and she stopped to help each driver. She called for a tow truck when necessary and made sure that everyone was okay before she continued on her way.

Finally, as the sun began to set, Mrs. Wilson returned home. She was exhausted but happy, knowing that she had done her part to help her community. She took off her coat and hat, poured herself a cup of tea, and sat down at her kitchen table.

As she sipped her tea, she looked out the window at the snow-covered world outside. She felt grateful for her job and for the chance to make a difference in the lives of the children she transported. She knew that being a school bus driver wasn't just a job, it was a responsibility, and she took that responsibility seriously.

Exercise

Select 3 words which are new for you in the story and make sentences in your own words.

1) ____

2) ____

3) ____

Identify 2 adjectives and 2 adverbs used in the story.

Adjectives: ______________ ______________ ______________

Adverbs: ______________ ______________ ______________

Write 3 sentences about the main character in your own words.

1) ____

2) ____

3) ____

What was the main idea of the story?

Reply:____

____

What was the problem faced by the main character in the story? How was it resolved?

Reply:____

____

Find two examples of similes or metaphors used in the story. Explain what they mean.

Reply:____

____

If you were the author, how would you change the ending of the story? Why?

Reply:____

____

____

____

The Classmate

Sophie had always been a quiet student. She sat at the back of the classroom, never raising her hand or speaking unless spoken to. She didn't have many friends, and she often felt like she didn't belong.

One day, a new student named Alex joined Sophie's class. Alex was outgoing and friendly, and he quickly made friends with everyone. Sophie was intrigued by Alex, but she was too shy to approach him.

As the weeks went by, Sophie watched as Alex interacted with her classmates. He was always smiling and making jokes, and he seemed to have a talent for making people feel comfortable.

One day, Sophie found herself sitting next to Alex in class. She was nervous at first, but Alex was friendly and easy to talk to. They started chatting, and before she knew it, Sophie found herself opening up to him. She told him about her struggles in school, her fears, and her dreams.

Alex listened patiently and then shared some of his own struggles with Sophie. He told her that he had moved around a lot as a child and had a hard time making friends. He said that he had learned to be outgoing as a way to cope.

Sophie and Alex continued to talk every day after that. They sat together in class, ate lunch together, and even worked on projects together. Sophie felt like she had found a true friend, someone who accepted her for who she was.

One day, as they were walking home from school, Alex turned to Sophie and said, "You know, Sophie, I'm really glad we became friends. You have a lot to offer, and I think you're going to do great things in life."

Sophie was taken aback by the compliment. She had never thought that anyone would see anything special in her. But hearing Alex's words made her feel like anything was possible.

Years later, Sophie looked back on that day as a turning point in her life. She realized that sometimes, all it takes is one person to believe in you, to see your potential, and to help you see it too. And for Sophie, that person was her classmate, Alex.

Exercise

Select 3 words which are new for you in the story and make sentences in your own words.

1) ____

2) ____

3) ____

Identify 2 adjectives and 2 adverbs used in the story.

Adjectives: ________________   ________________   ________________

Adverbs: ________________   ________________   ________________

Write 3 sentences about the main character in your own words.

1) ____

2) ____

3) ____

What was the main idea of the story?

Reply:____

____

What was the problem faced by the main character in the story? How was it resolved?

Reply:____

____

Find two examples of similes or metaphors used in the story. Explain what they mean.

Reply:____

____

If you were the author, how would you change the ending of the story? Why?

Reply:____

____

____

____

The Rose Garden

Lila had always loved roses. She loved their delicate petals, their sweet fragrance, and the way they bloomed in the sun. So when she inherited a piece of land from her grandmother, Lila knew exactly what she wanted to do with it.

She spent months researching the perfect rose varieties, studying the soil and the climate, and planning every detail of her dream rose garden. Finally, the day arrived when she was ready to begin.

Lila put on her gardening gloves and dug her first hole. She carefully planted the first rose bush, tucking the roots into the soil and covering them with earth. She watered the plant, and then moved on to the next one.

Hours turned into days, and days turned into weeks, but Lila never tired of working in her rose garden. She tended to each plant with love and care, pruning them, fertilizing them, and making sure they had enough water and sunlight.

As the summer wore on, Lila's rose garden blossomed into a riot of color. There were pink roses and red roses, yellow roses and white roses, each one more beautiful than the last. The garden was filled with the sweet scent of roses, and bees buzzed around the blooms, collecting nectar.

One day, as Lila was sitting in her garden, admiring her handiwork, a young woman walked up to her. "Excuse me," the woman said, "but I just wanted to tell you how beautiful your rose garden is. It's like walking through a fairy tale."

Lila smiled and thanked the woman. They struck up a conversation, and Lila learned that the woman had just moved to town and was feeling a bit homesick. Lila invited her to come back anytime she wanted, to sit in the garden and enjoy the beauty of the roses.

From that day on, Lila's rose garden became a sanctuary for many people in the town. People would come and sit among the roses, taking in their beauty and their fragrance. Some would even bring books or picnics and spend the whole afternoon in the garden.

Lila was overjoyed to see how her rose garden had brought joy to so many people. She realized that her love of roses had created a place of beauty and peace, a place where people could find solace and comfort in the midst of a busy world. And for Lila, that was the greatest gift of all.

<h3 style="text-align:center">Exercise</h3>

Select 3 words which are new for you in the story and make sentences in your own words.

1) ____

2) ____

3) ____

Identify 2 adjectives and 2 adverbs used in the story.

Adjectives: ______________   ______________   ______________

Adverbs: ______________   ______________   ______________

Write 3 sentences about the main character in your own words.

1) ____

2) ____

3) ____

What was the main idea of the story?

Reply:____

____

What was the problem faced by the main character in the story? How was it resolved?

Reply:____

____

Find two examples of similes or metaphors used in the story. Explain what they mean.

Reply:____

____

If you were the author, how would you change the ending of the story? Why?

Reply:____

____

____

____

The Railway Station

The railway station was always bustling with activity. Trains arrived and departed every hour, carrying people to and from distant places. The station was a hub of activity, a place where dreams were born and goodbyes were said.

One day, a young man named Jack arrived at the station. He was carrying a backpack and a guitar case, and he looked around nervously, as if he didn't know where to go.

A woman approached him and asked if she could help. Jack told her that he was a musician, and that he was hoping to catch a train to the next town, where he had a gig that night. But he had never been to the station before, and he wasn't sure where to find the right platform.

The woman smiled and led Jack to the platform he needed. She wished him luck with his gig and told him to enjoy the ride.

As Jack waited for his train, he watched the people around him. There were families with young children, businessmen in suits, and elderly couples with suitcases. Everyone seemed to be going somewhere, doing something, living their lives.

Finally, Jack's train arrived. He boarded the train and found a seat by the window. As the train pulled out of the station, he strummed his guitar and sang softly to himself. He was on his way to the next town, to share his music with a new audience.

As the train rattled along the tracks, Jack looked out the window and watched the world go by. He saw fields and forests, rivers and mountains, and towns and cities. He saw people going about their lives, each one with a story to tell.

When he arrived at his destination, Jack got off the train and made his way to the club where he was playing. He set up his equipment and began to play. The audience listened intently, swaying to the rhythm of his music.

After the show, Jack packed up his gear and headed back to the station. As he waited for his train, he realized that the railway station was more than just a place to catch a train. It was a place of stories and adventures, of dreams and goodbyes, of new beginnings and bittersweet endings. And Jack knew that he would always feel at home in the station, no matter where his travels took him next.

Exercise

Select 3 words which are new for you in the story and make sentences in your own words.

1) ____

2) ____

3) ____

Identify 2 adjectives and 2 adverbs used in the story.

Adjectives: ________________ ________________ ________________

Adverbs: ________________ ________________ ________________

Write 3 sentences about the main character in your own words.

1) ____

2) ____

3) ____

What was the main idea of the story?

Reply:____

____

What was the problem faced by the main character in the story? How was it resolved?

Reply:____

____

Find two examples of similes or metaphors used in the story. Explain what they mean.

Reply:____

____

If you were the author, how would you change the ending of the story? Why?

Reply:____

____

____

____

The Shopkeeper

Mr. Patel was the shopkeeper of a small convenience store located in the heart of a bustling town. His shop was always crowded, with people coming in and out all day long to buy groceries, snacks, and other essentials.

Mr. Patel had been running the shop for many years, and he knew most of his customers by name. He took pride in his store and made sure it was always well-stocked and clean. He was friendly and kind to everyone who came in, always ready to offer a smile and a helping hand.

One day, a young woman named Sarah walked into the shop. She was new in town and didn't know anyone. She had just moved into an apartment nearby and needed some groceries. Mr. Patel greeted her warmly and helped her find everything she needed. He also gave her some helpful tips about the town, telling her where to find the best restaurants, parks, and shopping areas.

Over the next few weeks, Sarah became a regular at Mr. Patel's shop. She would stop in every few days to buy something, and Mr. Patel would always greet her with a smile and ask how she was doing. He was like a friendly neighbor, always there to lend a helping hand.

One day, Sarah came into the shop looking upset. She had lost her job and didn't know how she was going to pay her bills. Mr. Patel listened sympathetically and offered her some advice. He told her that he knew a few people who were looking for workers and gave her their contact information.

Sarah was grateful for Mr. Patel's help, and she soon found a new job. She continued to shop at his store and they became good friends. Mr. Patel would always ask her how her job was going and how she was adjusting to life in the town.

Years went by, and Mr. Patel's shop remained a fixture of the town. It continued to serve the community with its friendly service and well-stocked shelves. Sarah eventually moved away, but she always remembered the kindness of Mr. Patel, the shopkeeper who had welcomed her to town and helped her when she was in need. She knew that he was more than just a shopkeeper, he was a true friend.

Exercise

Select 3 words which are new for you in the story and make sentences in your own words.

    1) ____

    2) ____

    3) ____

Identify 2 adjectives and 2 adverbs used in the story.

Adjectives: _______________ _______________ _______________

Adverbs: _______________ _______________ _______________

Write 3 sentences about the main character in your own words.

    1) ____

    2) ____

    3) ____

What was the main idea of the story?

Reply:____

____

What was the problem faced by the main character in the story? How was it resolved?

Reply:____

____

Find two examples of similes or metaphors used in the story. Explain what they mean.

Reply:____

____

If you were the author, how would you change the ending of the story? Why?

Reply:____

____

____

____

The River

The river flowed steadily through the countryside, winding its way past hills and valleys. The water was crystal clear, and fish could be seen darting in and out of the rocky bottom. It was a place of peace and tranquility, a natural haven from the hustle and bustle of the nearby town.

On the riverbank, a young boy named Tom sat fishing. He had come to the river with his grandfather, who had taught him how to fish and had spent many happy hours with him by the water. But today, Tom was on his own, and he was determined to catch the biggest fish he could.

As he sat there, waiting patiently for a bite, Tom noticed something strange. Upstream, he saw a log floating down the river. But this wasn't any ordinary log. It was a person, a young girl, who was clinging onto the log for dear life. She was screaming for help, and Tom knew he had to act fast.

He quickly reeled in his line and ran downstream to where he knew there was a shallow area in the river. He waded in, the cold water biting at his legs, and waited for the girl to come closer. As she floated past, he reached out and grabbed her, pulling her to safety.

The girl was shivering with cold and shock, but she was unharmed. She introduced herself as Lily and told Tom that she had fallen into the river while out on a hike. Tom took her back to his grandfather's cabin, where they warmed up by the fire and had some hot cocoa.

Over the next few days, Tom and Lily became good friends. They explored the countryside together, swam in the river, and fished for hours on end. Tom's grandfather was pleased to see him making new friends and enjoying himself so much.

As the days passed, Tom and Lily realized that they had fallen in love. They knew they would have to say goodbye soon, as Lily's family was moving away. But they made a promise to each other, that they would come back to the river every year and spend time together, reliving their memories and making new ones.

Years later, Tom and Lily did just that. They returned to the river, now with their own children in tow, and told them the story of how they had met. The river had been the backdrop for their love story, a place of beauty and wonder that had brought them together. And it would always hold a special place in their hearts.

Exercise

Select 3 words which are new for you in the story and make sentences in your own words.

1) ____

2) ____

3) ____

Identify 2 adjectives and 2 adverbs used in the story.

Adjectives: _______________   _______________   _______________

Adverbs: _______________   _______________   _______________

Write 3 sentences about the main character in your own words.

1) ____

2) ____

3) ____

What was the main idea of the story?

Reply:____

____

What was the problem faced by the main character in the story? How was it resolved?

Reply:____

____

Find two examples of similes or metaphors used in the story. Explain what they mean.

Reply:____

____

If you were the author, how would you change the ending of the story? Why?

Reply:____

____

____

____

The Oxen

In a small village, nestled at the foot of a great mountain range, there lived a farmer named John. John was known throughout the village for his strong and healthy oxen, which he used to plow his fields and transport goods to the market in the nearby town.

One day, as John was tending to his crops, he noticed that his oxen had grown tired and weak. They had been working hard for years, and it was beginning to take a toll on their health. John knew he had to do something to help his faithful companions, so he set out to find a solution.

He traveled to the town, seeking the advice of the local veterinarian. The veterinarian examined the oxen and advised John to give them a break from their work, to let them rest and recuperate. He also suggested that John feed them a special diet, rich in nutrients and vitamins, to help them regain their strength.

John took the veterinarian's advice and began to treat his oxen with the utmost care. He gave them plenty of time to rest, allowing them to graze in the lush fields surrounding his farm. He also prepared special meals for them, using only the finest ingredients and supplements.

As the weeks went by, John began to notice a change in his oxen. They had regained their strength and vitality, and they were once again eager to work. John felt a sense of pride and gratitude towards his oxen, realizing that he had taken their hard work for granted for too long.

From that day on, John treated his oxen with the respect and care they deserved. He knew that without them, he could not provide for his family, and he was grateful for their tireless efforts in helping him succeed. The oxen had taught him a valuable lesson, that hard work and dedication deserve to be rewarded with kindness and compassion.

Exercise

Select 3 words which are new for you in the story and make sentences in your own words.

    1) ____

    2) ____

    3) ____

Identify 2 adjectives and 2 adverbs used in the story.

Adjectives: ______________   ______________   ______________

Adverbs: ______________   ______________   ______________

Write 3 sentences about the main character in your own words.

    1) ____

    2) ____

    3) ____

What was the main idea of the story?

Reply:____

____

What was the problem faced by the main character in the story? How was it resolved?

Reply:____

____

Find two examples of similes or metaphors used in the story. Explain what they mean.

Reply:____

____

If you were the author, how would you change the ending of the story? Why?

Reply:____

____

____

____

The School Uniform

Lena had always been an independent girl, with her own sense of style and individuality. But when she transferred to a new school, she found herself faced with a strict dress code that required all students to wear a uniform.

At first, Lena was resistant to the idea. She felt that the uniform was a symbol of conformity, and that it would stifle her creativity and self-expression. But as she started to settle into her new school, she began to notice something interesting.

Despite the fact that everyone was wearing the same uniform, each student had found their own unique way to make it their own. Some students wore colorful socks or funky hair accessories, while others personalized their backpacks or decorated their school supplies.

Lena started to see the uniform as a canvas, a blank slate that she could use to express her own unique style. She experimented with different accessories, finding ways to make the uniform feel more like her own.

As she began to make friends and get involved in school activities, Lena realized that the uniform was actually a unifying force. It brought students together, helping them feel like they were part of a larger community. And even though everyone was wearing the same thing, there was still room for individuality and self-expression.

By the end of the school year, Lena had come to appreciate the uniform. It had taught her a valuable lesson about the power of unity and the importance of finding ways to express oneself within the confines of the rules. She had discovered that even when we are required to conform, there is still plenty of room for creativity and individuality.

Exercise

Select 3 words which are new for you in the story and make sentences in your own words.

    1) ____

    2) ____

    3) ____

Identify 2 adjectives and 2 adverbs used in the story.

Adjectives: ______________ ______________ ______________

Adverbs: ______________ ______________ ______________

Write 3 sentences about the main character in your own words.

    1) ____

    2) ____

    3) ____

What was the main idea of the story?

Reply:____

____

What was the problem faced by the main character in the story? How was it resolved?

Reply:____

____

Find two examples of similes or metaphors used in the story. Explain what they mean.

Reply:____

____

If you were the author, how would you change the ending of the story? Why?

Reply:____

____

____

____

The Accident

It was a beautiful summer day, and Emma was driving her car down the winding country road, enjoying the scenery. She had just graduated from college and was excited about her new job in the city. But her excitement turned to horror when she suddenly lost control of her car and skidded off the road, crashing into a tree.

When Emma woke up, she was lying on the ground beside her car, dazed and disoriented. Her head was pounding, and her body was wracked with pain. She tried to move, but every inch of her body felt like it was on fire.

As she lay there, she heard the sound of sirens in the distance. Help was on the way, but Emma knew that her life would never be the same. She had been in a terrible accident, and she was lucky to be alive.

Over the next few weeks, Emma struggled to recover from her injuries. She had broken several bones and suffered a traumatic brain injury, which left her with memory loss and difficulty concentrating. She had to learn to walk again, and she had to relearn even the most basic tasks, like tying her shoes or brushing her teeth.

Despite the physical and emotional pain she endured, Emma refused to give up. She worked tirelessly with her physical therapists and doctors, determined to regain her strength and independence. She also received emotional support from her family and friends, who rallied around her during her time of need.

Slowly but surely, Emma began to make progress. She regained her ability to walk, and her memory began to improve. She started to work again, and eventually returned to the city and her job. And although she would always carry the scars of her accident with her, she knew that she had been given a second chance at life, and she was determined to make the most of it.

Exercise

Select 3 words which are new for you in the story and make sentences in your own words.

    1) ____

    2) ____

    3) ____

Identify 2 adjectives and 2 adverbs used in the story.

Adjectives: _______________ _________________ __________________

Adverbs: _______________ _________________ __________________

Write 3 sentences about the main character in your own words.

    1) ____

    2) ____

    3) ____

What was the main idea of the story?

Reply:____

____

What was the problem faced by the main character in the story? How was it resolved?

Reply:____

____

Find two examples of similes or metaphors used in the story. Explain what they mean.

Reply:____

____

If you were the author, how would you change the ending of the story? Why?

Reply:____

____

____

____

The Morning Walk

Every morning, John took a walk around his neighborhood before starting his day. It was a peaceful time for him to clear his mind and enjoy the fresh air. But one morning, as he was walking down a quiet street, he noticed a small stray dog following him.

At first, John was hesitant. He didn't know the dog, and he didn't want to get too close. But as he continued his walk, he noticed that the dog was wagging its tail and seemed friendly. So, he decided to stop and say hello.

To his surprise, the dog ran up to him and jumped into his arms. It was a small brown and white terrier, with big brown eyes that seemed to look up at John with gratitude. John couldn't resist the dog's friendly demeanor, so he decided to take it with him on his walk.

As they continued down the street, John noticed that the dog seemed to be leading him in a particular direction. It would stop and sniff around certain areas, and then eagerly continue on. John followed the dog's lead, curious about where it was taking him.

Finally, they arrived at a small park on the outskirts of the neighborhood. John had never been there before, but the dog seemed to know it well. It ran up to a bench and sat down, looking up at John with a happy expression.

As John sat down next to the dog, he realized that this was exactly where he needed to be. He had been feeling lost and aimless, unsure of his direction in life. But this little dog had led him to a place of peace and serenity, a place where he could think and reflect on his life.

From that day on, John made it a habit to take his morning walk with the little stray dog. It became a ritual that brought him joy and purpose, and he knew that he had found a loyal friend in this small creature. And although he never knew where the dog had come from or where it went after their walks, he was grateful for the moments they shared together.

Select 3 words which are new for you in the story and make sentences in your own words.

    1) ____

    2) ____

    3) ____

Identify 2 adjectives and 2 adverbs used in the story.

Adjectives: ________________ ________________ ________________

Adverbs: ________________ ________________ ________________

Write 3 sentences about the main character in your own words.

    1) ____

    2) ____

    3) ____

What was the main idea of the story?

Reply:____

____

What was the problem faced by the main character in the story? How was it resolved?

Reply:____

____

Find two examples of similes or metaphors used in the story. Explain what they mean.

Reply:____

____

If you were the author, how would you change the ending of the story? Why?

Reply:____

____

____

____

The Junk Food

Lena had always loved junk food. She would eat chips, candy, and soda every day, despite knowing that it wasn't good for her health. Her friends and family had tried to persuade her to eat healthier, but Lena couldn't resist the delicious taste of her favorite snacks.

One day, Lena started feeling sick. She had a headache and stomach pains that wouldn't go away. Her doctor told her that her diet was the cause of her health problems, and that she needed to change her eating habits if she wanted to get better.

Lena was devastated. She had never thought that her love of junk food could lead to such serious health problems. But she knew that she needed to make a change if she wanted to feel better.

So, Lena began a new diet, filled with fruits, vegetables, and lean proteins. At first, it was difficult for her to give up her favorite snacks, but she was determined to stick to her new healthy lifestyle.

As time passed, Lena began to feel better. Her headaches and stomach pains disappeared, and she had more energy than ever before. She realized that her love of junk food had been holding her back, and that a healthier diet was the key to a better life.

Now, Lena still enjoys the occasional treat, but she knows that everything is best in moderation. She is grateful for the wake-up call that her health scare gave her, and she is happy to have a new lease on life.

Exercise

Select 3 words which are new for you in the story and make sentences in your own words.

    1) ____

    2) ____

    3) ____

Identify 2 adjectives and 2 adverbs used in the story.

Adjectives: ________________ ________________ ________________

Adverbs: ________________ ________________ ________________

Write 3 sentences about the main character in your own words.

    1) ____

    2) ____

    3) ____

What was the main idea of the story?

Reply:____

____

What was the problem faced by the main character in the story? How was it resolved?

Reply:____

____

Find two examples of similes or metaphors used in the story. Explain what they mean.

Reply:____

____

If you were the author, how would you change the ending of the story? Why?

Reply:____

____

____

____

The Barber

There was a small barber shop in the heart of the city that had been owned by the same family for generations. The current owner, Mr. Patel, had inherited the business from his father and had been running it for over thirty years.

Mr. Patel was known throughout the city for his excellent haircuts and friendly demeanor. He had a loyal customer base who came to him every week for a trim and a chat. And although the shop was small and simple, it had a certain charm that kept customers coming back year after year.

One day, a new customer walked into the shop. He was a young man with long hair, and he asked Mr. Patel to cut it all off. Mr. Patel was surprised, as he had never seen such a dramatic haircut request before. But he took it in stride and began to work on the young man's hair.

As he cut away the long locks, Mr. Patel noticed that the young man was nervous and fidgety. He tried to make small talk to ease his customer's nerves, but the young man remained silent.

Finally, the haircut was finished, and Mr. Patel handed the young man a mirror to inspect his new look. The young man looked at himself in the mirror and smiled. He thanked Mr. Patel and left the shop.

Weeks went by, and Mr. Patel didn't see the young man again. He assumed that the haircut had been a one-time thing and that the young man had found a new barber. But one day, the young man walked into the shop again, this time with a big smile on his face.

He told Mr. Patel that his new haircut had given him the confidence to go after his dream job. He had been hired as a graphic designer for a top company in the city, and he was on his way to fulfilling his lifelong dream.

Mr. Patel was thrilled to hear the young man's success story. He had always known that a simple haircut could have a profound impact on someone's life. And he was proud to be a part of the young man's journey to success.

From that day on, Mr. Patel continued to cut hair and listen to his customers' stories, knowing that each one had the potential to change someone's life for the better.

Exercise

Select 3 words which are new for you in the story and make sentences in your own words.

1) ____

2) ____

3) ____

Identify 2 adjectives and 2 adverbs used in the story.

Adjectives: _________________ __________________ __________________

Adverbs: _________________ __________________ __________________

Write 3 sentences about the main character in your own words.

1) ____

2) ____

3) ____

What was the main idea of the story?

Reply:____

____

What was the problem faced by the main character in the story? How was it resolved?

Reply:____

____

Find two examples of similes or metaphors used in the story. Explain what they mean.

Reply:____

____

If you were the author, how would you change the ending of the story? Why?

Reply:____

____

____

____

Forgiveness

Sophie sat alone in her room, staring at the wall, feeling angry and hurt. Her best friend, Emily, had betrayed her trust by telling everyone a secret that Sophie had confided in her. Sophie couldn't believe that Emily would do something like that.

Sophie decided to confront Emily about what had happened. She called Emily, and after a few minutes of arguing and shouting, Emily finally apologized. She told Sophie that she was sorry and that she didn't mean to hurt her. But Sophie was still angry and hurt, and she didn't feel like she could forgive Emily so easily.

Days went by, and Sophie still couldn't shake off the feeling of betrayal. She avoided Emily and refused to talk to her. But as time went on, Sophie started to realize that holding onto anger and resentment was only hurting her, and she decided to forgive Emily.

Sophie called Emily and told her that she forgave her. Emily was surprised but grateful. She apologized again and promised never to betray Sophie's trust again.

Sophie felt a sense of relief wash over her. Forgiving Emily had lifted a weight off her shoulders. She realized that forgiveness was not just about letting go of anger and hurt, but it was also about rebuilding trust and strengthening relationships.

Sophie and Emily's friendship slowly began to mend. They talked and laughed together, and Sophie felt like she had regained a sense of trust in Emily. She knew that forgiving her was the right thing to do, and that it had allowed her to move forward and grow as a person.

From that day on, Sophie understood that forgiveness was not a sign of weakness, but a symbol of strength and maturity. And she promised herself that she would always strive to be a forgiving person, no matter how hard it might be.

Exercise

Select 3 words which are new for you in the story and make sentences in your own words.

    1) ____

    2) ____

    3) ____

Identify 2 adjectives and 2 adverbs used in the story.

Adjectives: _______________ _______________ _______________

Adverbs: _______________ _______________ _______________

Write 3 sentences about the main character in your own words.

    1) ____

    2) ____

    3) ____

What was the main idea of the story?

Reply:____

____

What was the problem faced by the main character in the story? How was it resolved?

Reply:____

____

Find two examples of similes or metaphors used in the story. Explain what they mean.

Reply:____

____

If you were the author, how would you change the ending of the story? Why?

Reply:____

____

____

____

Breakfast

Emma woke up to the sound of her alarm clock beeping, signaling the start of a new day. She rubbed her eyes and sat up, feeling a bit groggy from a late night of studying. As she stumbled out of bed and made her way to the kitchen, she knew that a good breakfast would be the perfect way to start her day.

Emma's mother was already in the kitchen, sipping her morning coffee and reading the newspaper. "Good morning, sleepyhead," she said with a smile.

"Good morning, Mom," Emma replied, yawning.

"What would you like for breakfast today?" her mother asked.

"I think I'll have some scrambled eggs and toast, please," Emma said.

Her mother got to work, cracking the eggs into a bowl and whisking them together with a fork. She poured them into a hot pan and stirred them gently until they were perfectly cooked. She toasted some bread and spread a little butter on it.

As Emma sat down at the kitchen table, her mother brought her a plate of hot scrambled eggs and toast. Emma breathed in the delicious aroma and took a bite. The eggs were fluffy and creamy, and the toast was crispy and buttery.

"This is perfect, Mom," Emma said, smiling.

"I'm glad you like it," her mother replied.

They sat in comfortable silence, enjoying their breakfast together. Emma felt grateful for this simple moment, for the delicious food and the company of her mother.

As they finished their meal, Emma's mother reminded her to eat well and take care of herself, especially with exams coming up. Emma nodded, promising to try her best.

With a full stomach and a warm heart, Emma left for school, feeling ready to take on the day. She knew that no matter what challenges lay ahead, she could face them with a good breakfast and the support of her loved ones.

Exercise

Select 3 words which are new for you in the story and make sentences in your own words.

1) ____

2) ____

3) ____

Identify 2 adjectives and 2 adverbs used in the story.

Adjectives: ______________ ______________ ______________

Adverbs: ______________ ______________ ______________

Write 3 sentences about the main character in your own words.

1) ____

2) ____

3) ____

What was the main idea of the story?

Reply:____

____

What was the problem faced by the main character in the story? How was it resolved?

Reply:____

____

Find two examples of similes or metaphors used in the story. Explain what they mean.

Reply:____

____

If you were the author, how would you change the ending of the story? Why?

Reply:____

____

____

____

The Parrot

Once upon a time, there was a beautiful, colorful parrot named Polly. Polly lived in a big, luxurious cage in a large mansion owned by a wealthy family. The family was very fond of Polly and took great care of her. They loved listening to her talk and mimic their words, which made them laugh and entertained them.

One day, however, the family had to go on a long vacation and left Polly alone in the house with a caretaker who would come and feed her daily. Polly missed the family dearly and became lonely, and she longed for someone to talk to.

One day, a thief broke into the mansion, hoping to find valuable things to steal. When the thief saw the beautiful parrot in the cage, he was thrilled. He realized he could make a fortune by selling the parrot to a pet store or a collector. The thief stole the cage and the parrot and took them with him to his hideout.

Polly was terrified at first, but then she decided to use her ability to mimic words to her advantage. She began talking to the thief, telling him jokes and stories, and even singing songs. The thief was amazed by her skills and began talking back to her.

As the days went by, Polly and the thief became friends. They talked to each other every day, and Polly started to understand the thief's situation. He was a poor man who had been struggling to make ends meet and had turned to theft out of desperation.

One day, the family returned home, and the caretaker found that the parrot was missing. The family was devastated and offered a reward to anyone who could find their beloved pet. The thief realized that he could not keep Polly and decided to return her to the family, hoping to receive the reward.

When the thief brought Polly back, the family was overjoyed. They hugged Polly and thanked the thief for returning her. The thief accepted the reward but refused to take it, saying that he was happy to see the family reunited with their beloved pet. The thief realized that stealing was not the right thing to do and decided to turn his life around.

From that day on, Polly became a more talkative and cheerful parrot. The family loved her even more and appreciated her even more. Polly had made an unlikely friend in the thief, and they both learned a valuable lesson about the importance of friendship and forgiveness.

Select 3 words which are new for you in the story and make sentences in your own words.

1) ____

2) ____

3) ____

Identify 2 adjectives and 2 adverbs used in the story.

Adjectives: _______________ _______________ _______________

Adverbs: _______________ _______________ _______________

Write 3 sentences about the main character in your own words.

1) ____

2) ____

3) ____

What was the main idea of the story?

Reply:____
____

What was the problem faced by the main character in the story? How was it resolved?

Reply:____
____

Find two examples of similes or metaphors used in the story. Explain what they mean.

Reply:____
____

If you were the author, how would you change the ending of the story? Why?

Reply:____
____
____
____

Printed by Books on Demand GmbH, Norderstedt / Germany